D. MOWATT

HISTORIC

COMMUNITIES

The Gristmill

Bobbie Kalman

Crabtree Publishing Company

Created by Bobbie Kalman

For Joan, John, Brian,
and Heather Fryd

Editors
Marni Hoogeveen
Christine Arthurs

Design
Heather Delfino

Pasteup
Adriana Longo

Published by
Crabtree Publishing Company

1110 Kamato Road	350 Fifth Avenue	73 Lime Walk
Unit 4	Suite 3308	Headington
Mississauga, Ontario	New York	Oxford 0X3 7AD
Canada L4W 2P3	N.Y. 10118	United Kingdom

Cataloguing in Publication Data

Kalman, Bobbie, 1947-
 The gristmill

(Historic communities)
ISBN 0-86505-486-X (bound) ISBN 0-86505-506-8 (pbk.)

1. Flour-mills - History - Juvenile literature. 2. Grain - Milling - Juvenile literature. 3. Frontier and pioneer life - Juvenile literature. I. Title. II. Series: Kalman, Bobbie, 1947- . Historic communities.

TS2130.K33 1990   j664'.72272

Contents

Our daily bread

What could be better than a slice of homemade bread with butter?

Have you ever smelled bread baking in the oven? Nothing smells more delicious! No matter how full you are, it is hard to turn down a slice of freshly baked bread with butter. In this part of the world, most people eat bread at least once a day. We eat toast for breakfast, sandwiches for lunch, and sometimes have bread on the table at dinnertime. That is why bread is called a **staple**, or main food.

A life-sustaining food

The main ingredient of bread is flour. Flour comes from the grains of cereals such as wheat, corn, rye, and oats. These cereals contain important vitamins and fiber that our bodies need. The early settlers also needed the nutrition in bread to keep them healthy. They called bread "life-sustaining" because they believed that it kept them alive.

A very important story

Before settlers could bake bread, they first had to make flour. They could not buy flour at a store. They had to grind it from grain that they grew on their land. The story of grinding grain into flour is what this book is all about. In the days of the settlers, it was a very important part of daily life.

In the days of the settlers, there were many kinds of gristmills. Some were powered by wind; others by water. The type of gristmill we talk about in this book is a simple mill that was powered by a water-wheel. Many settlers used this kind of mill for grinding grain into whole-wheat flour.

The hard work of grinding

The settlers used different methods of grinding grain. Some brought hand mills from their old homes and ground their grain in these tiny grinders. It took a long time to get enough flour for a single loaf of bread.

The mortar and pestle

One method the settlers learned from the Native People was using a large **mortar** and **pestle**. The mortar was like a deep bowl. It was made by hollowing out the stump of a tree with an ax or burning a hole inside it. The pestle, a heavy club, was carved from a piece of hardwood. It was used to pound grain that had been poured into the mortar. You can imagine what difficult work this must have been because grain is very tough and has to be smashed many times to be broken down into flour.

The quern

Another grinding device the early settlers used was a **quern**. A quern was made of two round, flat stones placed on top of each other. The upper stone was turned by a handle. The lower one did not move. Grain was poured into a hole in the center of the top stone. As the top stone turned, the grain was crushed between the two stones and was pushed out to the side.

A wooden barrel surrounded the stones. The flour collected in the space between it and the stones and poured out of the barrel's spout into a bucket.

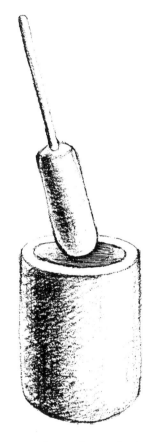

A mortar and pestle made from a tree stump and a piece of hardwood

Grain was carefully poured into the hole at the top of the quern, (opposite, top) and then ground between the stones (bottom, left).

(opposite, right) Both men and women took turns doing the tiring task of pounding grain using a mortar and pestle.

Building a gristmill

Grinding grain by hand was a tiring business. When enough people moved into an area, the settlers built a gristmill to ease their workload. "Grist" means grain, and a mill is something that grinds. Using special machinery, the gristmill ground grain into flour.

The best location

The first step in building a gristmill was finding the right location. The settlers searched for a spot on the banks of a fast-flowing, shallow river or by a waterfall. It was important to have a steady supply of water all year long. The best building site was located near a forest. The trees provided the wood needed to build the gristmill. They also soaked up moisture and prevented flooding.

Only the strongest logs were used to build a milldam because they had to stay in place even when there was a lot of rain. If the milldam broke, the whole mill could be washed away.

Working together

When a suitable location was found, everyone in the community cooperated in building the mill. The wood that was used to construct the building was cut right from the spot where the land was cleared for the mill.

The milldam and millpond

When the settlers built a gristmill beside a river or stream, they first created a millpond. This was done by building a dam across the river. The workers secured the logs carefully to the riverbanks to make sure the dam would not leak or break. When the dam was finished, the river or stream widened into a pond behind the dam. It became quite deep, too. Besides providing the gristmill with water to operate the mill, the millpond became a home for many fish and water birds.

Many hands were needed to construct the mill, which was often three stories high. The hard-working volunteers cheered loudly when the last beams went up.

The mill goes up

The early mills were built of wood or stone and looked like big barns. The **beams**, which formed the frame, were made of oak. Oak is a strong hardwood that the termite, a wood-eating insect, does not like. The logs were cut in such a way that they fit tightly together, and wooden **pegs** were used because nails were hard to get.

Some mills were three stories high. The third floor was used to store the grain and flour that the miller kept as payment for grinding the farmers' grain. The grinding was done on the floor below, and the bottom floor held the gears. The millwheel was either outside the building or inside the mill in a cagelike structure called a **wheel housing**.

This early mill was built more than three hundred years ago. It was powered by a waterwheel. The water came from the millpond, which was held back by the milldam. The miller, who became a wealthy man, owned much of the land around the mill. His large home can be seen behind the mill.

The miller

When a mill was built, the village needed a miller. The job was advertised in a nearby city or sometimes in faraway places. Some millers learned the skill of milling in Europe and came to work in North America.

The miller was a friendly man. Everyone in town used his services. He also brought his customers up to date on village news and gave them all kinds of advice.

The qualities of a good miller

The miller needed special knowledge to operate, adjust, and repair the millwheel, gears, and millstones. He had to know how to grind different types of grain without spoiling the flour. It was important for him to be in top physical condition because he had to carry around big bags of grain and flour! A good miller's senses were keen. He could tell by the rumblings of the wheels and gears if everything was working smoothly.

Hardworking and friendly

The miller was a hard worker. With so many settlers wanting their grain ground, he was usually at the mill from very early in the morning until late at night. A pleasant personality was important to the miller because almost everyone in the area was his customer.

A wealthy and respected man

The miller did not do his work for free. Instead, he received part of the flour he ground as payment for his work. He sold or traded his extra flour for food, goods, services, or land. Before long, the miller became the richest man in his community. Because many people admired the miller, it was natural for him to be elected to political office.

(left) The miller knew his machinery so well that he could tell what was wrong by listening to the sounds it made and by feeling the texture of the flour ground between the stones.

(bottom, left) The miller kept careful accounts of how much grain he ground for his customers.

(below) The miller's children did many chores around the mill. They swept the floors, helped unload the farmers' wagons, hitched up the horses, and looked after the mill cats. The miller's wife worked hard, too. She helped her husband serve customers and brought meals to him when he did not have time to eat with the rest of the family.

Waterwheels

W hy did the miller need a steady flow of water to operate his mill? The answer to this question is that he needed power. The settlers had no electricity to make their mills work. Instead, they used the waterwheel to turn the energy of water into the power needed to grind grain. The waterwheel was a huge wheel with paddles or buckets around its outside rim.

The undershot wheel

Several types of waterwheels were used. **Undershot** wheels were powered by swift-running streams or waterfalls. The speed of the water flowing underneath the wheel pushed the paddles and turned the wheel backwards.

The overshot wheel

The most efficient wheel was the **overshot** wheel. Its source of water was the millpond. From the millpond, water was carried to the mill through a channel known as a **millrace** and was directed to the top of the wheel through an open trough called a **sluiceway**. When the **sluicegate** was opened, the water spilled into the wooden buckets on the outside of the wheel. Even a small amount of water could operate an overshot wheel because the water in the top buckets was pulled down by gravity and forced the wheel to turn. As each bucket reached the bottom, it emptied and went to the top, where it was filled with water again.

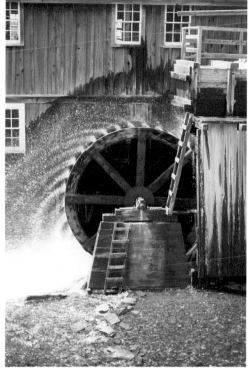

Are the three waterwheels shown in these photographs undershot or overshot wheels?

(bottom) The miller controlled the amount of water that reached the waterwheel by opening and closing the sluicegate.

The gears

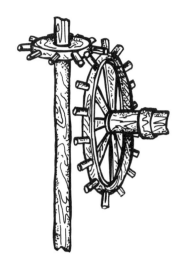

The first mills had gears made of wood. Whenever one of the teeth wore out or broke, the miller carved a new one and wedged it in place. In later times, gears were made of metal, so they lasted longer.

The waterwheel was a powerful piece of machinery. When it turned, the whole mill would shake and groan. The energy created by the wheel was used to grind the grain. But how was this energy passed on from the wheel to the millstones? The answer is **gears**.

Transferring energy

Two wheels with teeth made up the gears in an old gristmill. These teeth meshed with each other the way the teeth in a zipper do. As one wheel turned, it automatically turned the other. Gears transferred power from the source of energy, the waterwheel, to where the energy was being used, the millstones.

Pumped-up power

The gearwheel that was attached to the waterwheel was large, whereas the gearwheel that turned the millstone was one-fourth the size. Every time the large gearwheel turned once, the small one, which was connected to the millstone, spun four times. The millstone also spun four times, thereby grinding the grain more quickly.

Avoiding sparks

The movement of the gears involved many parts rubbing together, so there was always the danger that friction would produce sparks and start a fire. To avoid a disaster, the miller smeared animal fat on all the moving parts of the gears. The fat was melted by the heat created as the parts rubbed together. The liquid fat kept the gears turning smoothly.

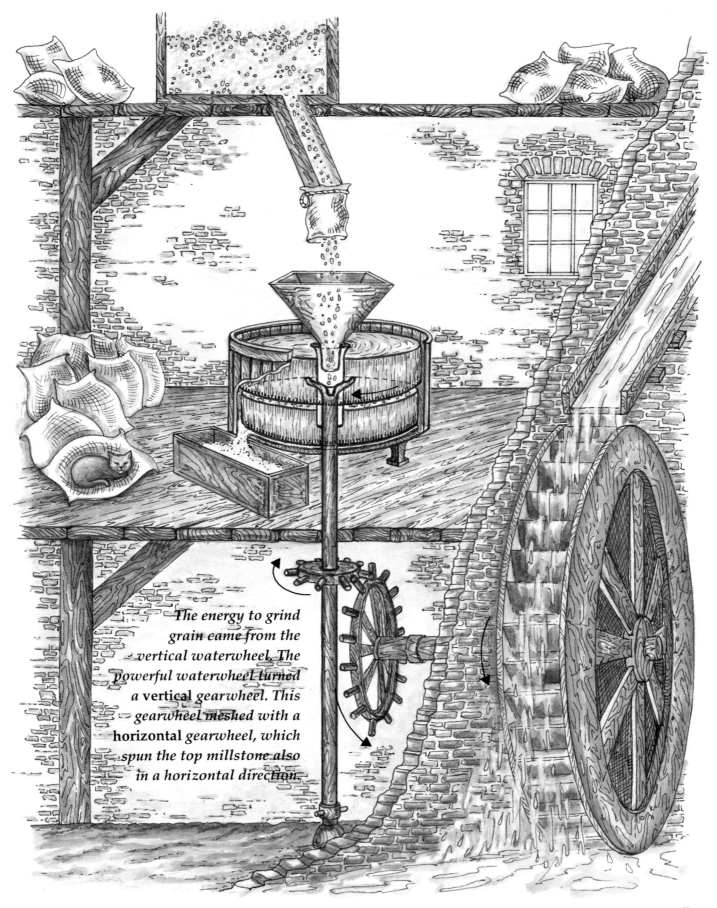

The energy to grind grain came from the vertical waterwheel. The powerful waterwheel turned a vertical gearwheel. This gearwheel meshed with a horizontal gearwheel, which spun the top millstone also in a horizontal direction.

The millstones

Grain was ground and crushed between a pair of huge, flat, round stones called millstones. They worked just like the stones in a quern. The millstones of the early mills were made at the mill site. In later times, these huge wheels were brought from other places. Because they were so heavy, they arrived in sections and had to be put together at the mill.

The two stones that worked together were known as a **run.** The bottom stone, or **bedstone,** did not move. A **stonespindle** passed through the hole in its center, was attached to the stone on top, called the **runner**, and made it turn.

The millstones were covered by a wooden structure called a **hoop.** *It kept the flour from flying all over the room. The flour was pushed out from between the stones and poured into a bin through a hole in the hoop. Then it was put into burlap sacks.*

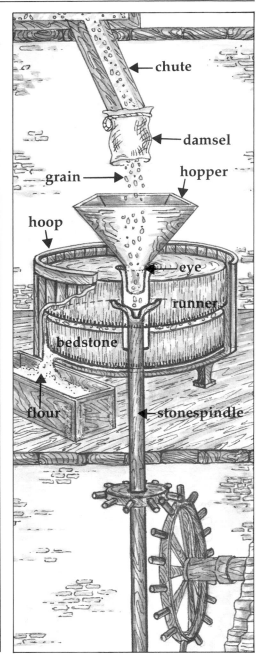

The right distance apart

The distance between the two stones was set according to the type of grain being ground. For example, wheat needed less space than corn for grinding. The miller had to make sure that the stones never touched. If they did, the flour would spoil and, what was worse, there was danger of an explosion because the flour could catch fire.

Grain was poured into a large bin on the third floor. It fell down a wooden chute and through the **damsel** *into a large funnel called the* **hopper.** *The hopper funneled the grain through a hole, called the* **eye,** *in the center of the runner. This top millstone turned about fifteen times a minute.*

The miller knew by the feel of the flour between his thumb and fingers if his machinery was running properly. This skill came to be known as the "rule of thumb."

All sorts of patterns were carved into millstones. The grooves, called furrows, pushed the flour out to the edges of the stones.

land   furrow

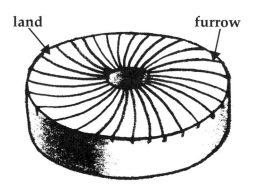

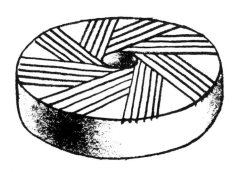

Stone furrows

The surface of each millstone had flat areas called **land** and a special design of grooves carved into it called **furrows**. In farming, furrows are the grooves made in the land by a plow. Both the land and the furrows ground the grain, but the furrows did three other things. They ripped off the grain's outer husk, directed the ground flour to the outside of the wheel, and allowed air to pass through the stones to let out the heat created during grinding.

The miller at this early mill dresses the millstones himself. In other villages, a dresser did this job. A dresser was sometimes asked to "show his mettle," or the small pieces of stone that were buried under his skin. This evidence proved to the miller that the dresser had a lot of experience. This expression is still used today. It means "to show one's worth."

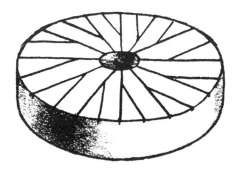

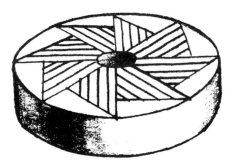

Dressing the millstones

Every few weeks the millstones needed to be "roughed up" or **dressed**. Both the land and the furrows wore down from constant use. The land had to be made bumpy again, and the furrows cut deeper. The miller or a special artisan called a **dresser** hammered at the stone with an iron pick called a **mill bill.** Some of the tiny bits of stone that flew up were driven deep into the skin of his hands.

A spike

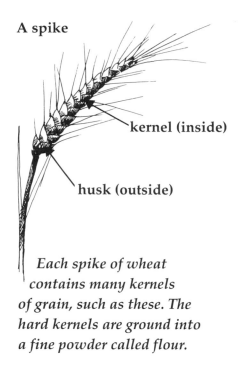

kernel (inside)

husk (outside)

Each spike of wheat contains many kernels of grain, such as these. The hard kernels are ground into a fine powder called flour.

Stalks of wheat were cut down with a scythe.

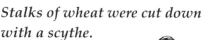

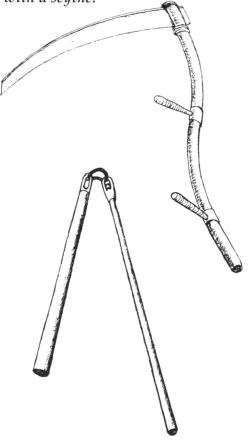

The flail was used to thresh wheat.

The story of wheat

Flour was usually made from wheat. Wheat is a cereal grass with a slender stalk, long, thin leaves, and a **spike** containing twenty to a hundred **kernels** of grain. Each kernel is covered by a protective coating called a **husk**.

Taking in the harvest

In the days of the settlers, stalks of wheat were cut down with **scythes** and tied in bundles. Using **flails**, the wheat was pounded in order to separate the kernels from the plants. The pounding also loosened the husks so that they would easily come away from the grain. Beating the wheat in this way was called **threshing**. After the wheat was threshed, the kernels were thrown up into the air. The wind caught the husks and blew them away, leaving the cleaned grain behind. This process was known as **winnowing**.

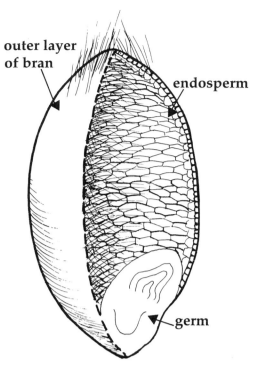

outer layer
of bran

endosperm

germ

(above) The endosperm is the largest part of the grain. It is the part from which white flour comes. White flour has almost no nutritional value. The wheat germ contains the growing power of the seed—the oil. It makes up only a tiny portion of the grain, but it is the most nutritious portion. The bran is the outer layer of the grain. It provides fiber, which is essential for good health.

(top, left) Before grinding, the kernels had to be separated from the husks. The farmers threw the grain into the air, allowing the husks to fly away in the wind. This was called winnowing.

Every kernel of grain has three different parts: the bran, the germ, and the endosperm. When all three parts of the grain are ground together, the result is whole-wheat flour. It is very nutritious.

(bottom) The settlers baked whole-wheat bread, which is brown, because the flour from which it was baked contained all three parts of the grain.

Getting grain to the mill

When grain was ready for grinding, the settlers faced the difficult task of getting it to the mill. Few roads existed at first. Many settlers walked long distances to the gristmill on footpaths through the forest. These journeys often took several weeks! Some farmers waited until winter so they could bring their grain to the gristmill by sleigh. In winter, travel was much less difficult because sleighs could glide easily over snow and ice even in places where there were no roads.

No matter how long it took the settlers to reach the gristmill, they considered the trip worthwhile. "Stone-ground" flour, which was the flour ground by millstones, was much better than the flour ground at home. The settlers were happy to travel almost any distance rather than grind grain by hand.

The farmers often brought grain to the mill in winter, when travel was less difficult.

Problems at the mill

This ground hog has been caught in the act! Animals often got into the flour and grain in search of a tasty and nutritious meal.

The mill cat was useful as well as friendly. The miller relied on it to keep mice and rats from over-running the mill.

The miller had a full-time job keeping the mill free of pests that wanted to eat his grain. Some of his worst enemies were mice, rats, ground hogs, weevils, moths, beetles, and mites. Mice and rats chewed through the bags to get at the grain and flour. Insects lived right in the flour. Almost every mill had at least one cat. These furry felines helped the miller keep the pests under control.

Fire

Fire was the miller's major worry because flour catches fire easily. Sparks from gears or millstones rubbing together sometimes started fires. The miller was always careful that the millstones never touched and the gears were kept well oiled. Even the flame of a candle could cause a disaster.

Floods

The other big danger the miller faced was flooding. If it rained too much and the river swelled, the extra pressure of the water could break the milldam. The tremendous force of the rushing water could wash the mill away.

Accidents

Besides fires, floods, and pests, millers had to be careful of accidents. Many millers lost their arms and legs while climbing under the waterwheels to free them from ice. It was also easy to fall off the top of a waterwheel.

Children climbed all over the millwheel when it was not in use and sometimes hurt them- selves. Other settlers drowned in the pond in summer or fell through the ice in winter.

A village is born!

Settlers from near and far traveled to the gristmill. When they arrived, others were often lined up ahead of them, waiting to have their grain ground. The tired travelers had to wait several hours to get their flour.

A general store opens

At first there was no place for the customers of a new gristmill to wait. Then one of the settlers saw a good business opportunity and opened a general store where travelers could rest, eat a meal, and get supplies. They could also trade their extra flour and farm products for other goods. The general store soon became a popular gathering place.

A growing community

After the general store was established, a blacksmith was next to open shop. Other craftspeople also set up workshops and, before long, new people began to settle in the area. Roads were put in, houses were built, and churches were erected. A new village was born!

Fun at the millpond

The millpond that formed behind the milldam was a place for fun. In summertime, villagers went fishing and swimming in the cool water and had picnics on the shore. In winter, the millpond made a great skating rink.

Glossary

account - A record of money paid and owed

artisan - A skilled craftsperson

burlap - A coarse, woven fabric made from hemp or jute

cereal - A grass that produces edible grain

community - A group of people who live together in one area and share buildings, services, and a way of life. A community is also the place in which these people live.

early settler - A person who is among the first people to settle in an area. A settler from an early time in history. A pioneer

energy - Usable power

feline - An animal from the cat family

fiber - Roughage; food that helps waste move through the intestines

gear - A wheel with teeth around its edge that meshes with the teeth of another wheel. Gears transfer power from one part of a machine to another.

general store - The main store in a settler community. It carries many kinds of supplies for trade or sale.

goods - Items that are made to be sold

grain - The hard seeds of a cereal plant

gravity - The pull towards earth that makes things fall

historic - Important in history. Historic places are important because they teach us how the people who settled this continent lived in the past.

horizontal - Having a position that runs from side to side

mettle - Strength of character; an old way to spell metal

millrace - A channel that brings water to a waterwheel

nutrition - Nourishment for the body

paddle - A broad board on a waterwheel that scoops water

peg - A thick wooden nail

power - A source of energy; strength

quern - A hand mill with two large stones used for grinding grain

rim - The outer edge of a wheel

scythe - An old-fashioned farming tool used for cutting down grass and wheat

service - Work done for others that does not produce goods

settler - A person who makes his or her home in a new country or part of a country that is not built up

site - The position or location of something

sluicegate - A large vertical board on the sluiceway that is used to control the flow of water to the waterwheel

sluiceway - An open trough through which water pours onto an overshot wheel

stonespindle - The rod attached to a gear at one end and the top millstone at the other. It turns the millstone.

vertical - Having a position that runs from top to bottom

winnow - To use wind to blow away husks from grain

Index

Acknowledgments

Cover photograph:
Metro Region Conservation Authority.

Title page photograph:
Metro Region Conservation Authority.

At Black Creek Pioneer Village:
Marc Crabtree: p.5, 13(top), 18, 19, 21, 23(bottom), 26(bottom); Metro Region Conservation Authority: p.4, 7(top and bottom left), 12, 13(bottom right), 15(bottom), 16, 20, 28-29.

At Saint-Marie Among the Hurons:
Jim Bryant: p.26(top); Bob Mansour: p.7(bottom right).

At Upper Canada Village:
Jim Bryant: p.9, 13(bottom left); Upper Canada Village-The St. Lawrence Parks Commission: p.23(top).

Other photographs:
W. Stephen Cooper, first printed in *Watermills of Ontario, Quebec, and Maritime Canada*, 1988. p.14; Bob Mansour: 15(top), 22.

Illustrations:
Cover: John Mantha; Halina Below-Spada: p.16(detail), 17, 19(detail); John Mantha: p.22(top), 23, 27(colorized etching); Metro Region Conservation Authority/Roblin's Mill Black Creek Pioneer Village, Bruce Milne, photographed by Sam Coates: p.30; The Harry T. Peters Collection of the Museum of the City of New York, The Mill-dam at "Sleepy Hollow": p.10-11 and Winter in the Country "The Old Grist Mill": p.24-25; National Archives of Canada/ C-21959, Erecting the Mill Dam, E. N. Kendall: p.8; David Willis: p.6, 15, 20-21, 22(bottom).

1 2 3 4 5 6 7 8 9 Printed in U.S.A. 9 8 7 6 5 4 3 2 1 0